RACIAL JUSTICE IN AMERICA
INDIGENOUS PEOPLES

The AMERICAN INDIAN MOVEMENT

HEATHER BRUEGL

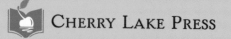

Published in the United States of America by Cherry Lake Publishing Group
Ann Arbor, Michigan
www.cherrylakepublishing.com

Reading Adviser: Beth Walker Gambro, MS, Ed., Reading Consultant, Yorkville, IL
Cover Art: Felicia Macheske
Produced by Focus Strategic Communications Inc.

Photo Credits: © fckncg/Alamy Stock Photo, 5; © Everett Collection Historical/Alamy Stock Photo, 7; © Teko Photography, 9, 30; © Lifes_Sunday/Shutterstock, 11; © ASSOCIATED PRESS, 12, 13, 21, 22, 28; Courtesy of Kisha James, 17; © The Patriot Ledger-USA TODAY NETWORK, 19; National Park Service, 25; Library of Congress, Prints and Photographs Division, 26

Cherry Lake Press is an imprint of Cherry Lake Publishing Group.

Library of Congress Cataloging-in-Publication Data

Names: Bruegl, Heather, author.
Title: The American Indian Movement / Heather Bruegl.
Description: Ann Arbor, Michigan : Cherry Lake Publishing, [2024]. | Series: Racial justice in America: Indigenous peoples | Audience: Grades 7-9 | Summary: "The social movements that defined the mid-20th century had lasting impacts on American society. This book takes a look at the American Indian Movement and how its activism brought much-needed attention to the injustices Indigenous Americans faced. The Racial Justice in America: Indigenous Peoples series explores the issues specific to the Indigenous communities in the United States in a comprehensive, honest, and age-appropriate way. This series was written by Indigenous historian and public scholar Heather Bruegl, a citizen of the Oneida Nation of Wisconsin and a first-line descendant Stockbridge Munsee. The series was developed to reach children of all races and encourage them to approach race, diversity, and inclusion with open eyes and minds"— Provided by publisher.
Identifiers: LCCN 2023043603 | ISBN 9781668939017 (paperback) | ISBN 9781668937976 (hardcover) | ISBN 9781668940358 (ebook) | ISBN 9781668941706 (pdf)
Subjects: LCSH: American Indian Movement—Juvenile literature. | Indians of North America—Government relations—1934— Juvenile literature. | Indians, Treatment of—United States—Juvenile literature.
Classification: LCC E93 .B8864 2024 | DDC 323.1197—dc23/eng/20231012
LC record available at https://lccn.loc.gov/2023043603

Cherry Lake Publishing would like to acknowledge the work of the Partnership for 21st Century Learning, a Network of Battelle for Kids. Please visit Battelle for Kids online for more information.

Printed in the United States of America

Note from publisher: Websites change regularly, and their future contents are outside of our control. Supervise children when conducting any recommended online searches for extended learning opportunities.

Heather Bruegl, Oneida Nation of Wisconsin/Stockbridge-Munsee is a Madonna University graduate with a Master of Arts in U.S. History. Heather is a public historian and decolonial educator and travels frequently to present on Indigenous history, including policy and activism. In the Munsee language, Heather's name is Kiishookunkwe, meaning sunflower in full bloom.

CHAPTER 1

What Is the American Indian Movement?

The 1960s in the United States was a time of change and a turning point in the fight for **equality**. The civil rights movement helped inspire the efforts of other minority groups to be heard. These groups demanded laws that protected their rights. From the civil rights battle to women's rights, people were willing to protest and were even willing to go to jail, if necessary, to stand up against injustices. This was also true for Indigenous people across the United States.

The American Indian Movement created a new space for Indigenous people to demand the government honor their rights, which were stripped away during colonization. The American Indian Movement gave a voice to a sometimes voiceless population, and the impact of its work can still be felt today.

The American Indian Movement, or AIM, focused on issues within Indigenous communities. These issues included sovereignty, treaties, education, racism, and police brutality. The group's purpose was to help Indigenous people living in cities.

The colors of the AIM movement represent the four cardinal directions. These colors are shared by Ojibwe and Lakota tribal groups: black/west, yellow/east, white/north, and red/south.

AIM was founded in Minneapolis, Minnesota, in July of 1968. The founders of AIM included Dennis Banks and Clyde Bellecourt. Banks was from Minnesota and had attended Indian boarding schools. He joined the U.S. Air Force when he was 19 years old. Banks became dependent on alcohol, struggled to make money, and was eventually arrested for burglary in 1966.

Banks met Bellecourt in prison. Bellecourt was born on the White Earth Reservation in Minnesota and had attended a Mission boarding school. Bellecourt also struggled to earn a living and, like Banks, was arrested for burglary. While in prison, Bellecourt studied history. He and Banks met with other inmates to read about Indigenous history and talk about their struggles.

Dennis Banks, Ojibwe, was cofounder of the American Indian Movement.

Banks and Bellecourt, along with a boarding school friend of Banks named George Mitchell, formed AIM in 1968. At one of AIM's initial meetings, 200 people showed up.

Eventually, Russell Means joined AIM. Means was born on the Pine Ridge Reservation in South Dakota and had lived on several reservations as a young adult, searching for work. He became a prominent leader in AIM and was often the spokesperson for the group. He spoke

In 1953, the U.S. Congress stopped fulfilling many of its commitments to Indigenous people. It also removed legal protections from Indigenous lands in a policy called Termination. The Bureau of Indian Affairs began an urban relocation program. The program invited Indigenous people to move into big cities.

The government promised Indigenous people jobs, housing, and a better life. Thousands of Indigenous families moved to cities looking for opportunity. Instead, they faced extreme poverty, discrimination, and homelessness. They also lost tribal relationships and parts of their culture in the process. Those that returned to their reservations often felt like they didn't fit in anymore among their own people.

at important events and testified before U.S. Congress on Indigenous rights.

The American Indian Movement organized large protests across the United States. The protests brought attention to Indigenous issues within Indian Country. The movement became quite adept at using media coverage, allowing Indigenous protesters the chance to make their voices heard.

The American Indian Movement is still active today. Its flag can be seen at protests across the country.

CHAPTER 2

The Occupation of Alcatraz

Although not an official AIM protest, the Occupation of Alcatraz was a defining moment in the Indigenous rights movement. Alcatraz was a notorious prison located in San Francisco Bay. The prison closed in 1963.

The Bay Area's Indigenous peoples had been lobbying for a cultural center and a school. They wanted it to be placed on the island, as the prison was sitting empty and unused.

In October 1969, a fire destroyed San Francisco's American Indian Center. Following the fire, a local group of Indigenous protesters decided that they were done waiting and organized an occupation.

"If a one-day occupation by White men on Indian land years ago established squatters' rights, then the one-day occupation of Alcatraz should establish Indian rights to the island," said Mohawk activist Richard Oakes. The protest group called themselves Indians of All Tribes.

Alcatraz once housed famous criminals like Al Capone, Mickey Cohen, and Machine Gun Kelly.

On November 20, the protesters made their move under cover of night. Eighty-nine individuals sailed to Alcatraz Island and claimed it for all Indigenous peoples. They demanded that the federal government provide funds to create a university and cultural center at Alcatraz. They painted graffiti on the abandoned walls, which included sayings such as "Red Power" and "Custer had it coming." They painted a sign on the water tower that read "Peace and Freedom. Welcome."

The population on Alcatraz grew to more than 600 people. A police force was established that was satirically named the Bureau of Caucasian Affairs. They patrolled the shoreline, always on the lookout for intruders.

A Lakota, John Trudell, joined the American Indian Movement. Trudell broadcasted under the Radio Free Alcatraz radio banner. Many others supported the protesters, and some shipped supplies to the island. AIM sent people to Alcatraz to learn about the protest and to see its progress.

John Trudell stands by a teepee on Alcatraz Island in this 1969 photo.

The Indigenous protesters claimed that Alcatraz was theirs by right of discovery. This was the right European colonists used to claim Indigenous land. The protesters argued that if White settlers could claim Indigenous lands, then Indigenous peoples could claim White land.

The protesters issued a proclamation stating plans to build an Indigenous school, cultural center, and museum on Alcatraz Island. They also facetiously offered to buy the island for $24 in glass beads and red cloth. The sum of $24 was the supposed amount that Europeans paid the Lenape for the island of Manhattan.

By the beginning of 1970, life on the island of Alcatraz had changed. Many of the activists were students who were leaving the island to go back to school. The federal government did not think the occupation would end on its own, so it cut off the island's power.

Finally, on June 11, 1971, the government sent in heavily armed troops to end the occupation. The government claimed it was there to fix a lighthouse and a foghorn.

The occupation ended without creating much change, but it inspired many more Indigenous rights activists to organize protests across the country. Some of these protests included Plymouth Rock, the *Mayflower*, and Mount Rushmore.

The large population of urban Indigenous people from many different nations created their own communities. This was the beginning of **intertribal** cultural centers where various groups worked together to promote Indigenous well-being. The first American Indian Center in San Francisco ran from the 1940s to 1969 when it was burned down. The American Indian Center in Chicago is another such organization, which began in 1953 and is still active today.

CHAPTER 3

Plymouth Rock and the Trail of Broken Treaties

In 1970, a Thanksgiving celebration was planned in Plymouth, Massachusetts. It was the 350th anniversary of the Pilgrims' landing at Plymouth Rock. Wamsutta Frank James, an Aquinnah Wampanoag tribal member, was invited to speak to mark the occasion.

The theme of the day was brotherhood, but James' speech included some harsh truths. He said, "History gives us facts and there were atrocities." James also talked about the Wampanoag loss of culture, language, land, and life.

The organizers of the event would not let James give his speech. Instead, supporters from local tribes, United American Indians of New England (UAINE), and the Boston Indian Council followed James to Cole's Hill. They gathered next to the statue of former Wampanoag leader Ousamequin, also known as Massasoit, to hear James give his original speech.

Wamsutta Frank James speaks in front of the statue of Massasoit in 1970.

The speech was not entirely negative. James ended the speech with a call for unity and hope.

"You the White man are celebrating an anniversary. We the Wampanoags will help you celebrate in the concept of a beginning. It was the beginning of a new life for the Pilgrims. Now, 350 years later it is a beginning of a new determination for the original American: the American Indian."

AIM's national director Russell Means and other AIM activists attended and gave speeches at that Thanksgiving Day protest, too. They, along with others, buried Plymouth Rock under mounds of sand and climbed onto the replica of the *Mayflower* ship.

The police were called, and the protesters left the ship. James spoke to reporters, saying that though national groups and local groups disagreed on how to approach the day, all agreed that people needed to be made aware of Indigenous issues. UAINE and James' family have kept the protest alive for over 50 years.

Thanksgiving Day in 1970 was declared the first National Day of Mourning. Every year on that day,

Russell Means speaks following Wamsutta Frank James at the 1970
protest in Plymouth.

Indigenous people gather to remember all that was lost. Today, the National Day of Mourning is a day of remembrance and spiritual connection. It is also a day to protest the racism and oppression that Indigenous Americans continue to experience.

AIM did not organize the event, but the group's headline-grabbing approach at the time often sees them credited for the National Day of Mourning. Instead, credit belongs to Wamsutta Frank James and the UAINE. AIM was able to use the momentum and publicity of the event to grow its own influence.

By 1972, AIM had grown in influence. It was one of eight organizations that sponsored a cross-country march called the Trail of Broken Treaties. The march was held in the fall of that year, bringing attention to Indigenous issues such as poor living standards, lack of housing, and broken treaties.

In October, one group of protesters gathered in a caravan on the American West Coast and proceeded to head eastward. Two other caravans started at other points. They met in Minnesota. The joint caravan carried the Twenty-Point Position Paper and reached Washington, D.C., in November. The procession grew bigger as it traveled. In fact, so many people joined the caravan that there were not enough places to stay in Washington, D.C. People who had initially agreed to host protesters backed out as the caravan grew in numbers.

Hundreds of Indigenous activists occupied the Bureau of Indian Affairs at the end of the Trail of Broken Treaties.

The group decided to occupy the Bureau of Indian Affairs to help them have their demands heard. The occupation of the building was front page news for the *New York Times*. The organizers presented the Twenty-Point Position Paper and demanded legal rights for Indigenous people.

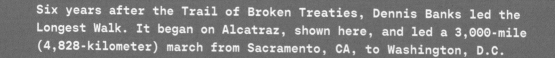

Six years after the Trail of Broken Treaties, Dennis Banks led the Longest Walk. It began on Alcatraz, shown here, and led a 3,000-mile (4,828-kilometer) march from Sacramento, CA, to Washington, D.C.

The Nixon Administration refused to meet with the protesters to receive the Twenty-Point Position Paper. After a week, protest leaders negotiated with government officials, bringing an end to the protest. These government officials promised to include Indigenous people in future treaty negotiations. It was an empty promise. The United States had stopped making treaties with Indigenous nations in 1871.

A selection of the protesters' demands from their Twenty-Point Position Paper:

- Restore Indigenous nations' right to make treaties.
- Create new treaties between the United States and Indigenous nations.
- Review treaty commitments and violations.
- Provide relief from treaty violations.
- Allow Indigenous nations to interpret treaties.
- Have Congress work to fix relationships with Indigenous nations.
- Return 110 million acres of land to Indigenous communities.
- Get rid of the Bureau of Indian Affairs.

CHAPTER 4

The Occupation of Wounded Knee

One of the last significant protests organized by AIM was the Wounded Knee Occupation. Wounded Knee is located on the Pine Ridge Reservation in South Dakota. It is a place of great historical significance.

In 1890, the U.S. Army had been forcing American Indigenous people onto reservations. Many Indigenous people fought against this enforcement agenda. They resisted and rejected White social norms. They embraced their own culture instead. At the heart of many conflicts in 1890 was the Ghost Dance.

Many Lakota believed that if they practiced the Ghost Dance, the gods would reward them with a new life off the reservations. They thought they had been confined to reservations because they had abandoned their ancient Indigenous ways.

On December 15, 1890, reservation police tried to arrest the famous Hunkpapa Lakota Chief Sitting Bull at the Standing Rock Reservation. The police falsely accused Sitting Bull of being a Ghost Dancer. Sitting Bull was killed by the arresting officers.

Four hundred fifty Lakota performing the Ghost Dance on the Pine Ridge Reservation in 1890.

Upon hearing about the death of Sitting Bull, Chief Spotted Elk (Big Foot) led 350 of his people to safety at the Pine Ridge Reservation. On December 28, the 7th Cavalry approached them and surrounded the group. The following morning, U.S. soldiers entered the camp to disarm the Lakota people.

A deaf Lakota man was reluctant to give up his rifle, claiming he had paid a lot for it, and the rifle accidentally discharged. The soldiers began to fire

These survivors of the Wounded Knee Massacre were photographed in 1891. A handwritten note on the image says "What's Left of Big Foot's Band."

into the crowd of Lakota people. Many tried to escape but were hunted down and shot, some as far as 2 miles (3.2 kilometers) away.

Between 150 and 300 Lakota were killed, with most of those being women and children. The U.S. Army referred to this massacre as the Battle of Wounded Knee, and 20 soldiers were awarded the Medal of Honor for their involvement.

In 1973, corruption was rampant on the Pine Ridge Reservation. Many individuals, including AIM co-founder Dennis Banks, sought the leadership of traditional leaders. They gained the most support on Pine Ridge, but they also angered the corrupt tribal chairman Dick Wilson, who had a lot of political control. The tribal council had charged Wilson with several items for an impeachment hearing.

There were other concerns at Pine Ridge, too. Many Indigenous people were murdered in towns next to the reservation, and no one was ever charged with the murders. Something had to be done, so the Elders called for AIM members to occupy the sacred ground of Wounded Knee.

On February 27, 1973, the occupation of Wounded Knee began. Protesters demanded that Wilson be removed from office. They also demanded immediate revival of treaty talks with the federal government. About 10 days into the occupation, roadblocks were set up to block people from entering the town and dropping off supplies. While the days were mostly quiet, there was nightly gunfire.

At one point during the occupation, the protesters declared themselves part of the Independent Oglala Nation and demanded to speak with the Secretary of State. Elder Frank Fools Crow and a small delegation went to the United Nations for recognition. They did not receive it, but the United Nations became increasingly more involved in the rights of Indigenous peoples.

The occupation of Wounded Knee ended on May 8, 1973, after 71 days. Despite this resolution, the violence in Pine Ridge continued. There were several further murders of Indigenous people in the region that many believed were committed by Wilson and those who worked for him.

The occupation of Wounded Knee in 1973 was not the last time Indigenous people organized and protested.

In 2016, Indigenous women organized resistance camps where Water Protectors lived and worked during Standing Rock protests to stop the Dakota Access Pipeline. The American Indian Movement still exists today, fighting for Indigenous rights. Indigenous peoples are still here, and their fight is unending.

Dennis Banks (left) and Carter Camp (right) read a government offer to end the occupation on March 18, 1973. They did not accept.

Standing Rock protesters demanded protection for Indigenous land and water. Indigenous people of all ages rallied to defend their rights.

Water Protectors of Standing Rock

The U.S. government approved construction of an oil pipeline called the Dakota Access Pipeline (DAPL), which would bring oil from Canada into the United States. The pipeline's path went through the Standing Rock Reservation and under Lake Oahe, an important water source for the reservation.

The Standing Rock Sioux Tribe opposed the pipeline. It threatened both their water supply and their land. They organized protests that were often led by youth groups. People camped near the construction site, and protesters clashed with police and private security. People from around the world showed their support for the protesters. These activists became known as Water Protectors, defending Indigenous life and land.

The DAPL was completed in 2017. Indigenous groups have since won several court cases against the government and the oil company involved. The legal battle to shut down the DAPL continues today.

EXTEND YOUR LEARNING

BOOKS

Bell, Samantha. *Thanksgiving: The Making of a Myth*. Cherry Lake Publishing, Ann Arbor, MI, 2024.

Loh-Hagan, Virgina. *Stand Up, Speak Out: Indigenous Rights*. 45th Parallel Press, Ann Arbor, MI, 2022.

Phillips, Katrina M. *Indigenous Peoples' Day*. Pebble, Rocheport, MO, 2022.

Quigley, Daw. *Inspiring Leaders: Native American Heroes*. Scholastic Book Clubs, New York, 2021.

WEBSITES

With an adult, learn more online with these suggested searches.

"American Indian Movement." Library of Congress.

"American Indian Movement (U.S. civil rights organization)." Britannica Kids.

"National Museum of the American Indian." Smithsonian.

GLOSSARY

caravan (KAIR-uh-van) a group that travels together during a long trip

equality (ih-KWAH-luh-tee) concerning the state of being equal

Ghost Dance (GOHST DANS) a dance believed to revive the dead and restore traditional ways of life

impeachment (im-PEECH-muhnt) to charge a public official with a legal wrongdoing

Indian Country (IN-dee-uhn KUHN-tree) self-governing communities throughout the United States

intertribal (in-tuhr-TRIE-buhl) shared across two or more tribes

lobbying (LAH-bee-ing) trying to influence public officials or a legislative body

occupation (ah-kyuh-PAY-shuhn) assuming control

Oglala Nation (ahg-LAH-luh NAY-shuhn) one of the seven bands of the Titowan division of the Lakota

relief (re-LEEF) unburdening; aid

replica (RE-pli-kuh) a close remake of the original

United Nations (yow-NIE-tuhd NAY-shuhns) political organization with representatives from many of the world's countries

violations (vie-uh-LAY-shuhns) to treat wrongly

INDEX